YUMA COUNTY LIBRARY DISTRICT

D0431888

DISCARDED
BY
Yuma County Library District

HOSTAGE RESCUE WITH THE SAS

ELITE FORCES SURVIVAL GUIDE SERIES

Elite Survival
Survive in the Desert with the French Foreign Legion
Survive in the Arctic with the Royal Marine Commandos
Survive in the Mountains with the U.S. Rangers and Army
  Mountain Division
Survive in the Jungle with the Special Forces "Green Berets"
Survive in the Wilderness with the Canadian and Australian
  Special Forces
Survive at Sea with the U.S. Navy SEALs
Training to Fight with the Parachute Regiment
The World's Best Soldiers

Elite Operations and Training
Escape and Evasion
Surviving Captivity with the U.S. Air Force
Hostage Rescue with the SAS
How to Pass Elite Forces Selection
Learning Mental Endurance with the U.S. Marines

Special Forces Survival Guidebooks
Survival Equipment
Navigation and Signaling
Surviving Natural Disasters
Using Ropes and Knots
Survival First Aid
Trapping, Fishing, and Plant Food
Urban Survival Techniques

HOSTAGE RESCUE
WITH THE SAS

CHRIS McNAB

Introduction by Colonel John T. Carney. Jr., USAF–Ret.
President, Special Operations Warrior Foundation

Yuma Co. Library Dist.
350 3rd Ave.
Yuma, AZ 85364
928-782-1871
www.yumalibrary.org

MASON CREST PUBLISHERS

This edition first published in 2003
by Mason Crest Publishers Inc.
370 Reed Road, Broomall, PA, 19008

© 2003 Amber Books Ltd.

All rights reserved. With the exception of quoting brief passages for the purposes of review, no part of this publication may be reproduced without prior written permission from the Publisher.

We recognize that some words, model names—and designations, for example—mentioned herein are the property of the trademark holder. We use them for identification purposes only. This is not an official publication.

Library of Congress Cataloging-in-Publication Data available

ISBN 1-59084-011-9

Editorial and design by
Amber Books Ltd.
Bradley's Close
74–77 White Lion Street
London N1 9PF

Project Editor Chris Stone
Designer Simon Thompson
Picture Research Lisa Wren

Printed and bound in Malaysia

10 9 8 7 6 5 4 3 2 1

ACKNOWLEDGMENT
For authenticating this book, the Publishers would like to thank the Public Affairs Offices of the U.S. Special Operations Command, MacDill AFB, FL.; Army Special Operations Command, Fort Bragg, N.C.; Navy Special Warfare Command, Coronado, CA.; and the Air Force Special Operations Command, Hurlbert Field, FL.

IMPORTANT NOTICE
The survival techniques and information described in this publication are for use in dire circumstances where the safety of the individual is at risk. Accordingly, the publisher cannot accept any responsibility for any prosecution or proceedings brought or instituted against any person or body as a result of the uses or misuses of the techniques and information within.

DEDICATION
This book is dedicated to those who perished in the terrorist attacks of September 11, 2001, and to the Special Forces soldiers who continually serve to defend freedom.

Picture Credits:
Corbis: 10, 38, 52 ; **Military Picture Library:** 21; TRH: 6, 12, 14, 16, 18, 22, 26, 30, 33, 34, 36, 37, 40, 44, 47, 48; /P.Valpolini: 8, 28.
Illustrations courtesy of Amber Books and the following supplied by Patrick Mulrey: 24, 42, 50, 53, 54, 56.
Front cover: **TRH** (inset), **Corbis** (main)

JUL 1 0 2003

CONTENTS

INTRODUCTION

Elite forces are the tip of Freedom's spear. These small, special units are universally the first to engage, whether on reconnaissance missions into denied territory for larger, conventional forces or in direct action, surgical operations, preemptive strikes, retaliatory action, and hostage rescues. They lead the way in today's war on terrorism, the war on drugs, the war on transnational unrest, and in humanitarian operations as well as nation building. When large scale warfare erupts, they offer theater commanders a wide variety of unique, unconventional options.

Most such units are regionally oriented, acclimated to the culture and conversant in the languages of the areas where they operate. Since they deploy to those areas regularly, often for combined training exercises with indigenous forces, these elite units also serve as peacetime "global scouts" and "diplomacy multipliers," a beacon of hope for the democratic aspirations of oppressed peoples all over the globe.

Elite forces are truly "quiet professionals": their actions speak louder than words. They are self-motivated, self-confident, versatile, seasoned, mature individuals who rely on teamwork more than daring-do. Unfortunately, theirs is dangerous work. Since "Desert One"—the 1980 attempt to rescue hostages from the U.S. embassy in Tehran, for instance—American special operations forces have suffered casualties in real world operations at close to fifteen times the rate of U.S. conventional forces. By the very nature of the challenges which face special operations forces, training for these elite units has proven even more hazardous.

Thus it's with special pride that I join you in saluting the brave men and women who volunteer to serve in and support these magnificent units and who face such difficult challenges ahead.

Colonel John T. Carney, Jr., USAF–Ret.
President, Special Operations Warrior Foundation

An SAS soldier of the Counter-Revolutionary Warfare (CRW) Wing uses the Remington 870 pump-action shotgun during an exercise.

THE BIRTH OF HOSTAGE-RESCUE UNITS

The murder of 11 Israeli athletes at the 1972 Olympic Games in Munich, Germany, prompted many Western governments to create special hostage-rescue units. In Britain, the SAS refined its hostage-rescue tactics to prepare for any eventuality.

Today, many countries face the threat of hostage-taking and terrorist attacks against their citizens. For this reason, many governments have established expert counter-terrorist units. Each unit is ready to be deployed at a moment's notice to combat the menace of hostage-taking. The American Special Forces have a secret force, the British have the Special Air Service (**SAS**), and other European countries have created their own elite teams.

There are currently more than 90 counter-terrorist/hostage rescue units (**CT/HRUs**) around the world. Many of these have been established and trained by the SAS and other leading CT units. The need for such units became apparent in the 1960s, when many international terrorist groups began to attack places and people around the world. These attacks ranged from bombings to hostage-taking. The incident above any other that led to the creation of Western counter-terrorist units was the horrible massacre of 11 Israeli athletes at the 1972 **Olympics**.

Elite troops have special training facilities for abseiling (see glossary). The Austrian GEK unit uses a 300-foot (91-m) tower at Wiener Neustadt.

On September 5, 1972, armed members of the Palestinian terrorist group "Black September" seized 11 Israeli athletes at the Olympic Village in Munich. They demanded the release from prison of 234 of their fellow terrorists. The terrorists and their hostages were flown by helicopter to Furstenfeldbruk military airport. From here they were promised they would be given safe passage to Cairo. However, as they left the helicopters, hidden snipers opened fire, killing two terrorists and wounding others, as well as two helicopter crewmen. The surviving terrorists managed to get back to the helicopters. In cold blood, they executed five of their

The helicopter is ideal for reaching remote locations. The SAS practice abseil drops from helicopters onto oil rigs in the icy North Sea off the coast of eastern England and Scotland.

hostages in one helicopter before blowing it up, while the other helicopter exploded in the firefight. Five terrorists were killed and three captured, but at the price of 11 Israeli hostages murdered.

The massacre sent shock waves throughout Western Europe and the United States. Munich had shown that local police forces, however well trained, could not hope to fight a determined terrorist attack. The necessity for dedicated hostage-rescue units was accepted, and plans to create them were quickly set in motion.

Only highly skilled individuals would be suitable for such units. Candidates would have to be excellent marksmen capable of using a variety of weapons, but also be good at negotiating and calming down the situation if possible. They would need to be fit and intelligent, capable of operating alone or in small groups.

On September 11, 2001, the fight against terrorism was stepped up in response to terrible atrocities in New York and Washington D.C which claimed the lives of more than 5,000 Americans. The following units continue to fight the terrorist menace.

Germany's GSG 9

West Germany's Grenzchutzgruppe 9 (**GSG 9**) was formed on September 26, 1972. To get into GSG 9 is very difficult. An initial interview selects candidates who are already good at police work. They must also be self-confident, intelligent, and have the ability to mix with other people from all walks of life, which prepares them for work as bodyguards. If they are picked, practical training lasts for four months. After that, they are put on standby in case of emergencies. The officers keep their skills sharp by practicing a

GSG-9 operators brace themselves for a fast entry through a door. They carry the 9-mm MP5 submachine gun made by Heckler & Koch.

series of simulated hostage-rescues from cars, trains, aircraft, boats, and buildings. Marksmanship skills are also constantly maintained to provide excellence. Each combat team fires in excess of one million rounds of ammunition a year. GSG 9 achieved an outstanding success in October 1977, when hostages being held in a Lufthansa Boeing 737 at Mogadishu Airport, Somalia, were rescued safely.

France's GIGN

France's crack hostage rescue unit is called Groupenment d'Intervention de la Gendarmerie Nationale (**GIGN**). France has

experienced many problems with terrorism and hostage-taking. That's why GIGN soldiers are among the best in the world.

After training and a successful period in the French police, candidates may apply to transfer to GIGN. Before candidates are interviewed, their past performance records are checked thoroughly to see if they are eligible for the job. All applicants have to complete basic parachute and diving courses before they can be selected for the training course. This training course emphasizes mental and physical fitness, strength, raw courage, and marksmanship. On average, GIGN agents fire 9,000 pistol rounds and 3,000 rounds of rifle ammunition on the firing range every year.

This GIGN sniper has a fast-rope and radio tied to his belt. He is wearing thermal imaging goggles.

Diver training continues in the unit, and the candidates progress to become combat swimmers, spending four hours a week underwater. Much of the training is conducted at night—the best time for the insertion of swimmers during a hostage-rescue operation is under cover of darkness. To help prepare the team for night diving, it sits at the muddy bottom of the River Seine, listening to the heavy barges passing overhead. This lets the individuals get used to the sound of passing ships, which appear larger and closer than they actually are.

The GIGN's expertise in swimming proved essential in May 1977 when combat swimmers were deployed during a train hijack. A Dutch train was seized by terrorists. Combat swimmers managed

The elite sniper rarely gets more than once chance to hit his target, so he must make sure that he does not hit a hostage.

COLONEL CHARLES BECKWITH

One of the most famous men in the world of elite forces is Colonel Charles Beckwith, who was an elite U.S. Special Forces soldier. He learned his skills from the SAS, training with them before going on to fight with them against guerrilla fighters in Malaya in the 1950s. He took these skills into the Vietnam War, where he fought with distinction in command of a specialist unit. After the Vietnam War ended, Beckwith went back to the U.S. In 1977 he was given a new job. He was asked to create a secret elite counterterrorist force. Beckwith kept a close relationship with the SAS, and the early training of the new unit's soldiers was even done by the SAS themselves.

to swim up a canal running close to the railroad track and attach heat detectors and listening devices to the outside of the train. These enabled the rescue planners to establish the precise whereabouts of the gunmen before the final assault.

The United States' Counterterrorist Force

Responsibility for hostage-rescue within the United States lies with the **FBI**, which maintains its own Hostage Rescue Unit (**HRU**). Known as the Hostage Response Team, the 50-strong unit is reputed to be among the best in the world. The FBI also has small counter-terrorist teams in each state. However, many hostage situations

A hostage-rescue unit bursts into a room. See how each soldier is responsible for checking a different area of the room. A terrorist could open fire at any moment so it is essential the unit works as a team.

involve criminals, not terrorists, and are usually dealt with by state, county, or city police Special Weapons and Tactics (**SWAT**) teams.

U.S. counterterrorist operations abroad, including hostage-rescue, are the responsibility of the Army's First Special Operational Detachment. It was formed by Colonel Charles Beckwith, a U.S. Special Forces veteran who had served with the British SAS in the early 1960s. All applicants for this unit must attend a lengthy and very difficult interview. They must also undergo psychological assessment before they are even accepted for selection. This mental evaluation ensures that they are mature enough to endure the endless waiting that often happens with hostage situations. The size

The SAS "buddy-buddy" system involves separating the soldiers into pairs; each looks out for the other in an amazing display of teamwork.

and organization of the unit is a closely guarded secret, although it is considered to have approximately 400 active personnel. Half of the staff are full combat operators and are divided into two squadrons.

Possibly the most famous of all hostage-rescue units is the British SAS. Though the SAS mainly take part in conventional military operations, its soldiers are also trained to complete fast and furious rescue actions. In the next chapter, we will look at how the SAS are trained in hostage-rescue missions. Then we will look at one of the most famous hostage-rescue incidents in history—the operation at the Iranian Embassy in London in 1980.

TRAINING WITH THE SAS

SAS soldiers spend hours simulating hostage-rescue situations. All elements of a hostage-rescue mission must go smoothly, because any mistakes might result in hostages being killed. There are no second chances.

At the SAS headquarters in Hereford, England, every member of the Regiment's Sabre Squadrons trains for hostage-rescue operations in a special building, known as the "Killing House."

Inside the Killing House, live ammunition is used all the time, though the walls have a special rubber coating that absorbs the impact of rounds as they hit. Before going into any hostage scenario, the team always goes through the potential risks they may face. The priority is always to rescue the hostages as quickly, but above all as safely, as possible. Sometimes, unfortunately, that can mean using lethal force against the people who are holding the hostages. Other times it can just mean talking the terrorists into surrendering—the best option for everyone.

Training in the Killing House involves bursting into a room, often filled with smoke. In only seconds the SAS trooper must identify who are the terrorists and who are the hostages. Both are played by cardboard cutouts, though sometimes other SAS soldiers sit in as hostages. The SAS trooper must either shoot the terrorists

The SAS is very secretive. Soldiers are not allowed to speak about their training and operations even after they have left the Regiment.

SAS soldiers training in the Killing House can expect to fire anything up to 2,000 rounds of ammunition each year during training.

or get the hostages out as quickly as possible. The aim is that all SAS members are trained up to the same level of skills. They must constantly think about what their colleagues are doing so the whole unit works as a team. The "House" is full of corridors, small rooms, and obstacles, and often the scenario demands that the rescue be carried out in darkness. This is because on a real mission the electric power is often cut off before the team goes into a building. The rooms are quite empty, but they can be laid out to resemble the size and layout of a real target, and the hostages will often be mixed in among the gunmen.

Confidence in using live ammunition is developed by using "live" hostages, who are drawn from the teams. (They wear body armor but no helmets.) They usually sit at a table or stand on a marked spot, waiting to be "rescued." The **CQB** (Close-Quarter Battle) range also includes electronically operated figures that can be controlled by the training staff. At a basic level, for example, three figures will have their backs to the soldier as he enters the room. Suddenly, all three will turn and one will be armed. In that split second, the soldier must make the right assessment and target the

During Continuation Training, SAS soldiers are taught abseiling, combat skills, survival techniques, jungle warfare, and escape and evasion.

correct person. If the soldiers do not do it quickly enough, it would probably mean death in a real hostage-rescue situation. A variety of situations can be developed by the instructors, using, for example, smoke, gas, obstacles to separate team members from their colleagues, as well as loudspeakers to simulate crowd noises and shouting. Speed, fast reactions, and slick drills are the key during hostage rescue. Four-person assault groups are normally split into two teams of two. Each person is given specific areas inside each room to clear.

An eight-man Special Air Service squad moments before boarding a Chinook helicopter and heading into enemy territory in Iraq for covert operations during the Gulf War in 1991.

By the late 1970s, the SAS could be confident that it was fully trained in hostage-rescue tactics. The Regiment had approached its new task with its usual combination of cool determination and tough training. It was confident that it could successfully tackle a hostage-rescue mission. However, there inevitably remained an element of doubt because the SAS's training had yet to be put to a practical test. There was, of course, only one method for testing their training. But first the Regiment had to assist an ally's hostage-rescue unit.

On October 13, 1977, four Palestinian terrorists hijacked a Boeing 737 airliner of the German national airline, Lufthansa. The leader of the terrorist group was Zohair Akache, a man who called himself "Captain Mahmoud." The hijackers had taken hostage the airliner, its five crew members, and 86 passengers. Their demands were the immediate freedom of 11 members of another terrorist organization who were being held in Germany.

The terrorists forced the airliner to fly to many different places. It finally arrived at Mogadishu in the Somali Republic, Africa. Following it was another German airliner, secretly carrying 30 men of the GSG 9 hostage-rescue unit. In addition, the aircraft carried two members of the SAS Regiment—Major Alastair Morrison and Sergeant Barry Davies. They were ready to give advice on tactics. In fact, the assault that finally took place was planned by the two Britons.

On October 16, Captain Mahmoud murdered the captain of the airliner. Inside the airliner, conditions were rapidly getting worse and worse, and Captain Mahmoud was becoming increasingly agitated. He set a deadline of 0255 hours (2:55 A.M.) on October 18 for the release of all the terrorists, with the threat that he would otherwise blow up the airliner. GSG 9 decided it was time to launch their attack.

At 0205 hours (2:05 A.M.), Somali soldiers lit a fire on the runway ahead of the airliner. This was intended to distract the terrorists inside the airliner. Two minutes later, the emergency doors over the airliner's wings and at the front and rear of its fuselage were all blown open by special explosive charges. **Stun grenades** were

Smashing through glass is a dramatic SAS method of entering a building, but the soldier's thick suit protects him from injury.

thrown into the fuselage—these hand grenades make a loud bang and flash, but do not really hurt people seriously. Then there followed a blinding flash and an extremely loud bang, and the four GSG 9 assault teams stormed into the airliner. An intense battle raged for the next five minutes as the West German soldiers fought with the terrorists. It was a hard battle, confusing and dangerous given its conditions within the confines of the airliner. However, the expertise of the GSG 9 soldiers soon resulted in all the hostages being freed and all the terrorists either dead or in captivity.

It was a superb operation, and though it had unfortunately ended in violence, almost all the hostages had been freed unhurt. The tactics of the SAS had paid off brilliantly. But before long, they had their own hostage-rescue mission to perform.

RULES FOR CLEARING BUILDINGS OF TERRORISTS

- Move as fast as possible and keep moving until the operation is finished.
- Do not stand still in doorways and corridors—you will be an easy target.
- When looking around a wall, peer around it at a level close to the ground. The enemy will not be looking for a human head at foot height.
- Cross open space only when a colleague is covering you.
- Attack from the top of the building down—you can move more quickly going down stairs than going up!

PRINCES GATE—PLANNING

On the morning of April 30, 1980, six armed terrorists launched themselves into the Iranian embassy at No. 16 Princes Gate in London and seized 22 hostages. The events that followed became one of the most famous and successful hostage-rescue operations in history.

The terrorists were armed with guns and grenades, and were very dangerous. They demanded the release of 92 Arabs from Iranian jails as well as safe passage out of Britain for themselves as soon as their demands had been met. They said that they would start killing the hostages if their demands were not met.

Police negotiators began the difficult task of calming the situation, talking to the terrorists over the telephone. At the same time, specialized police units began to arrive. These specialized units included police marksmen and antiterrorist officers. They were destined to be only supporting actors in the crisis, however, because the central players had yet to arrive.

An SAS team was sent immediately from Hereford, where a group is always on 24-hour standby in case of hostage-rescue and antiterrorist emergencies. This was called Red Team and comprised a captain and 24 troopers. Also at the scene was Lieutenant-Colonel Michael Rose, commander of the Regiment.

An SAS soldier prepares to go into action during the Iranian Embassy siege. The attack was launched from the roof of the building.

SAS training in the Killing House at Stirling Lines, Hereford. The barracks was named after the founder of the SAS, David Stirling.

Once at the scene, the SAS started to plan the hostage-rescue mission if it were needed. Red Team was several times put on full alert for a rapid assault when the terrorists made particular threats against the hostages. Fortunately, these turned out to be false alarms, though they made everyone very tense when they happened. Reinforcements arrived during the afternoon of May 2 in the form of SAS Blue Team. Negotiations between the police and the terrorists continued.

As they were doing so, both SAS assault teams studied every scrap of information about the Iranian embassy building.

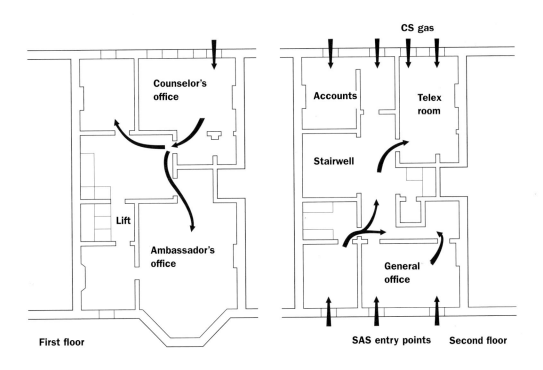

A diagram showing the route the SAS soldiers took through the first floor of the Iranian embassy. The soldiers all entered quickly through the windows of the building. They had cleared it 17 minutes later.

Microphones were installed by MI5, the British secret intelligence organization, in the walls and down the chimneys. This made it possible for the police and SAS to determine the location of the terrorists and hostages. At the nearby Regent's Park Barracks, British Army engineers built a full-scale model of the embassy. At government level, Prime Minister Margaret Thatcher discussed the crisis with the police and the military, including the SAS.

Time was nonetheless running out, however, for the government was refusing to meet the terrorists' demands. Ali Mohammed, code-named "Salim," the terrorist leader, began to sound increasingly aggressive and nervous as he spoke to police negotiators during May 5. And by early evening, matters had gone seriously wrong. Several gunshots were heard from inside the Iranian Embassy. Then the body of the embassy's chief press officer, Abbas Lavasani, was thrown onto the pavement outside the building. It was a horrible moment. The police leader telephoned the government to tell them that he was turning over command of the situation to the SAS. At 1907 hours (7:07 P.M.), the SAS formally took control. Operation "Nimrod" was now underway.

An SAS soldier involved in Nimrod talked about the build-up to going into action: "When we had arrived at the start of the siege, we had been told to be ready to storm the building within 15 minutes. This would mean going in and trying to reach the hostages before they were killed. At that stage, we had no idea where the hostages actually were. I looked at the embassy and thought of clearing 50 rooms one by one, while all the time looking out for the terrorists and their prisoners.

"However, because the negotiators kept the terrorists talking, we were given a few days in which to prepare ourselves. We spent the time finding out about every part of the building. The plan, like most good ones, was fairly simple: Red Team would enter and tackle the top half of the building, while Blue Team would clear the lower half of the embassy."

On the roof, Red Team waited to go into action. This involved the use of two teams, each with four men, to abseil from the roof to

A mock-up of a building used for hostage-rescue training. Elite forces training must be as realistic as possible to prepare soldiers for action.

the back balcony on the third story of the building; a third team to storm the fourth story, and a fourth team to blow in the skylight on the fifth story so its men could make their entry from the roof. Blue Team was given the tasks of clearing the basement, ground, and second floors. Red Team began the operation, but then nearly destroyed its chances just as it was beginning:

"We were on the roof waiting for the order to go. We had all made our last-minute checks and now we wanted to be off. The excitement was unbelievable. The word was given and we started to descend from the roof. Then, disaster. One of our men got caught up in his rope. Some of the others tried to help him, but then one of them accidentally broke a window with his foot."

The SAS have influenced many other elite units, including the Grupo Especial de Operaciones (GEO) of Spain. This soldier carries an MP-5 submachine gun.

KEEPING OPERATIONS SECRET

Before a hostage-rescue mission can take place, the elite unit needs to gain information about where the enemy is. This often means planting listening devices and miniature cameras in the walls. But this has to be done without letting the terrorists inside hear. One way of carrying out this operation is to arrange to have noisy construction work going on nearby—the noise covers the sounds of planting the surveillance devices. An amazing technique used during the Iranian Embassy siege was to get airliners to change their flight paths so that they flew low over the building. Every time the jets thundered over the embassy, the police would try to plant their surveillance devices.

A SAS soldier from Red Team hangs by his rope and throws a CS grenade during Operation Nimrod, May 5, 1980.

PRINCES GATE— INTO ACTION

After days of meticulous planning, the SAS soldiers were now ready to go. If they were to free the hostages unhurt, they would have to move with incredible speed through the corridors of the embassy. The SAS soldiers take up the story.

"All hell broke loose as orders were screamed to storm the building. Snipers started firing **CS gas** into the embassy. We couldn't get the other soldier free from his rope. Looking down, I saw the men from Blue Team using sledgehammers to break the glass and get in. The sound of gunfire filled the air as black-suited individuals started disappearing into the embassy. What chaos!"

At the front of the building, on the second-story balcony, a four-man SAS team placed a special explosive against the windows, but before it could be detonated, the men had to yell at one of the hostages to move farther back into the embassy, well away from the window. A few seconds later, there was a loud explosion.

"Then we were in. We threw in stun grenades and then quickly followed. There was a thundering bang and a blinding flash as the stun grenades went off. No one in here, good. I looked around; the stun grenades had set fire to the curtains, not so good. No time to stop and put out the fire. Keep moving. We swept the room, then

Two soldiers creep across the roof of No. 14 Princes Gate. Moments later, they abseiled into the Embassy, killing five terrorists.

An elite unit training in thick smoke. Colored smoke is used in combat to create confusion and conceal troops as they advance on the enemy.

heard shouts coming from another office. We hurried toward the noise, and burst in to see one of the terrorists struggling with a policeman who had been taken hostage. One of the team members rushed forward and got the policeman away, and then dealt with the terrorist. One down, five to go. We continued our search. The building was filling with CS gas and smoke. We had to free the hostages and get out as quickly as possible. Where were they?"

At first, it had been thought that the hostages were being held in an office at the rear of the building. The men of Red Team expected to find them there as the troopers smashed the glass and

During Princes Gate, the SAS wore fire-resistant assault uniforms and breathed using the S6 respirator, an earlier model of the S10.

then hurled in stun grenades. These rooms were empty, however. The leader of the SAS operation was still tangled in his rope, and flames were now starting to lick his legs as inflammable material inside the Iranian Embassy building caught fire. Fortunately, one of the second wave of abseilers cut the commander loose, and he crashed down onto the balcony. One of the SAS soldiers smashed a window and hurled a stun grenade into a room containing a

A hostage flees across the embassy using the balcony. The operation was a glowing success and the Prime Minister, Margaret Thatcher, rushed to congratulate the Regiment.

terrorist, causing the terrorist to run from the room. An SAS man chased the terrorist, who ran to the embassy's telex room. Here three other terrorists had just started to shoot at their hostages. The SAS troopers had to react swiftly and accurately:

"We heard the screams of the hostages coming from the telex room. 'They're killing them all,' I heard my mate shout. We raced into the room. It was chaos. One of the terrorists was shot straight away. We ordered everyone onto the floor. The terrorists had mixed themselves in with the hostages. The women were screaming as we started to bundle them out of the room. One terrorist was identified, pulled out of the line, and made to lie on the floor. Then he tried to throw a hand grenade, and we had to shoot him.

"Keep moving. We forced our way into other rooms and began clearing them. Shoot off the lock, kick in the door, stun grenade, wait for the bang, then in and clear it. Empty. Keep going, and so it went on. By this time it was getting difficult to see, as the building was filling with smoke and the CS gas. Then we received the order—building clear, hostages safe. Time to leave. I was caked in sweat and my mouth was parched, but I felt elated because the operation had clearly been a success."

The hostages and the one surviving terrorist were bound and secured on the lawn of the Iranian embassy so that each one could be positively identified. Five of the terrorists had been killed inside the embassy. Of the hostages, one had been killed and another injured by the terrorists during the course of the assault.

For the SAS, the whole operation was the clearest possible proof that its thinking and training concerning hostage-rescue

The inside of the embassy was badly damaged in the assault. Certain high explosives used by the SAS release huge gas shock waves, which destroy everything in their path.

operations was exactly right. But the aftermath was both good and bad for the SAS. One of those who took part describes the result of the siege:

"**Princes Gate** was a turning point. It demonstrated what the Regiment could do. But it also brought a problem we wanted to avoid: the media. In addition, for the first few years after the siege, SAS Selection courses were packed with what seemed like every man in the British Army wanting to join the SAS."

Despite these problems, the rescue at the Iranian embassy had shown the world what an elite hostage-rescue unit could do. Though it was undoubtedly the skills of the SAS soldiers that made the operation such a success, hostage-rescue squads are also helped by special equipment. This is what we will look at now.

WASHINGTON D.C. HOSTAGE RESCUE

Washington, D.C., is home to the president, U.S. government, and many important buildings and businesses. That is why it attracts people who want to commit acts of terrorism. One of Washington's most elite hostage-rescue teams is the police Emergency Response Team (ERT). This was created in 1984. Its officers are trained in all aspects of work relating to the security of the city. They have to be intelligent, very fit, expert with weapons, and highly trained in hostage-rescue techniques. To date, they have had to deal with many dangerous situations, and their quick responses have already saved many lives.

EQUIPMENT

Rescuing hostages from flame-filled buildings with enemy bullets flying around demands specialized equipment for hostage-rescue teams. These units therefore make sure they have the best clothing and equipment available to do the job.

If an SAS team has to make an assault on a terrorist-held building, it is faced with many problems, including heat, fire, blast, and smoke, not to mention bullets fired by the terrorists. The team seeks to surprise the terrorists or criminals. Then they have to move through the building as fast as possible to keep the terrorists confused and too poorly positioned to use their weapons. Every member of a rescue team, therefore, wears an assault suit and underwear made of flame-resistant material (which does not burn). The basic protection given by the assault suit can be increased as the situation demands by wearing items of assault underwear under the assault suit. It is standard to wear fireproof gloves to protect the hands and wrists. They also provide a good grip on equipment and weapons.

Hostage-rescue soldiers almost always wear body armor. Modern body armor is generally made from a material called **Kevlar**. This is a lightweight fiber of immense strength, strong enough to absorb the impact of bullets. The SAS uses Kevlar body armor with ceramic inserts to provide a high level of protection against all types of

The final part of SAS training involves a 40-mile (64-km) march over mountains in 20 hours with over 99 pounds (45 kg) of pack.

bullets. In a normal vest, the bullet may be prevented from reaching and penetrating the wearer. Yet it can still leave a dent in the armor so deep it can injure or kill the person wearing it. To get around this, another shield is worn under the vest, which takes out the energy from the bullet and protects the soldier even more, but the impact of the round may still knock down and wind the wearer.

Protection for the head is also an essential requirement for hostage-rescue troops. Normal military helmets are unsuitable for hostage-rescue soldiers. They are too heavy, not strong enough, and tend to become dislodged or skewed during the assault. Manufacturers therefore set about designing a lightweight helmet that could be worn over a gas mask, was difficult to knock off, offered a high level of protection, and helped prevent dust, tear gas, smoke, grit, and debris from getting into the eyes, nose, and mouth. The helmet currently used by the SAS is so strong that it can even stop certain bullets. It is comfortable and light to wear, so soldiers can use it easily during hostage-rescue operations.

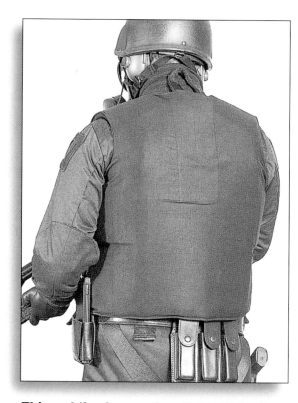

This soldier is wearing GPV 25 body armor with ceramic plates in the back.

SEEING IN THE DARK

When a hostage-rescue unit enters a building, it may be in total darkness. So how do they see? One way is to strap a flashlight along a gun. This helps the soldiers see exactly where they are aiming their weapons, and they can also dazzle their opponents with the bright beam. But there are more sophisticated devices. One is thermal imaging goggles. Thermal Imaging devices "see" heat instead of light. This means that people stand out warm against their background. It also means that people can even be seen hiding behind walls or other objects.

The nature of a hostage-rescue operation demands the utmost speed to throw the terrorists off balance and keep them in a disoriented state. For this reason, hostage-rescue units make extensive use of explosives, shotguns, and sledgehammers to get into buildings. Once inside, they use stun, CS gas, and smoke grenades as the assault team moves through the building. This means that the room or airliner fuselage will generally be filled with dust, debris, gas, and smoke. Also, flammable materials can catch fire. For this reason, it is standard procedure in a hostage-rescue operation to cut off the electricity and natural-gas supplies to an occupied building. Survival in these conditions can only be provided by wearing a **respirator**, a machine that lets people breathe even in thick smoke.

The respirator currently used by the SAS provides full protection for the eyes, nose, and mouth. It is also very easy to breathe through. Hostage-rescue operations can be exhausting and the soldiers need to breathe easily to keep their heads clear. The respirator protects against gases, aerosols, and smoke. The eyepieces will not mist up, and they are resistant to scratching and attacks by chemicals. They are often tinted black, and this, combined with the black color of the other clothing worn by each SAS hostage-rescue trooper, makes the soldier look very menacing. This is an intentional ploy because it helps to intimidate opponents and makes them more likely to surrender. The respirators also have built-in radio that make it very easy for the troopers to speak to each other during the confusion of a rescue mission.

In addition to proper clothing, hostage-rescue teams must have the equipment to let them gain entry to buildings, boats, and aircraft to reach the hostages. Fortunately, elite units such as GSG 9 have equipped their soldiers with a whole range of hostage-rescue equipment.

A hostage-rescue assault is generally launched from the roof of an occupied building. This offers the best chance of assembling the team in secrecy. An accurate and speedy arrival at a window or door from the roof is vital, and abseiling equipment is generally used for this purpose. This equipment comprises a rope, a harness to wear around the body, and something called a "descendeur." A descendeur connects the harness to the rope and lets the soldiers control how fast they go downward. It is hand-operated for pre-set slow, medium, or fast descents.

When they cannot abseil down to their entry point, the members of the assault team often have to climb up to it. In this situation, the assault ladder comes into its own. Assault ladders are made of lightweight aluminum so they are easy to carry around and use. Each rung of the ladder is deeply **serrated** to provide the best possible grip for the hand and foot, and also against walls and airliners. There is also a double-width ladder that can support six troopers at a time.

Other features include a hooked top for additional grip. The ladders can be carried on lots of different vehicles. They can also be used as bridges and can be clipped together into units of the

Soldiers from GEO, Spain's counterterrorist unit. They are armed with Heckler & Koch 9-mm submachine guns and handguns in holsters.

Hostage-rescue units have a number of ways to break down doors. One way is to shoot the locks off using special shotgun rounds.

right length. The SAS (together with other European special forces) keeps a record of the height of the windows of buildings that might be attacked by terrorists. They also know the measurements of the wings of the main airliner types, and the doors of airliners and trains. Assault ladders may seem a trivial item, but it was the silent placing of rubber-coated assault ladders against the fuselage of the hijacked Boeing 737 airliner at Mogadishu in October 1977 that played a significant part in the success of the GSG 9 operation.

Among the tools carried by the assault team can be a number of simple yet important items such as sledgehammers, bolt cutters, glass cutters, axes, wrecking bars, and grappling hooks.

One of the most useful tools for hostage-rescue units is the stun grenade, which was devised by the SAS. It is a special explosive that is not designed to kill, but instead explodes with a deafening bang and blinding flash to distract or incapacitate terrorists. It is now available in different types that can make one bang or many bangs. One type produces a loud bang as well as an intense light that lasts for 15 seconds. Another type of grenade issues eight loud bangs in quick succession. There is even another type that has no bang. Some have lots of bangs, produce loads of smoke, and flash many times.

The stun grenade is useful because hostage-rescue units prefer not to kill anyone—including terrorists—during a mission. It is much better if the terrorists can be brought to trial and justice. That is why the hostage-rescue units will try to get a hostage situation settled peacefully before any violent action is taken.

NEGOTIATION

Many hostage-rescue units have expert negotiators as part of their teams. They are trained to talk to hostage-takers and try to get them to surrender instead of fighting it out. It is a job that requires an ability to talk to people, and a lot of patience.

One of the first procedures for a hostage-taking situation is to get the negotiator in touch with the hostages. Usually this is done by telephone. If he or she can get the terrorists to talk to them, the negotiator will calmly and patiently reason with them. The priority is to calm the terrorists down, but also buy more time so that hostage-rescue teams can get themselves ready if they need to go into action. It is a difficult job. The terrorists will probably be aware that the negotiator is doing this, so a complex game of wits develops between the two parties. Most soldiers or police officers in hostage-rescue units are taught negotiation skills. Elite soldiers may be trained in these techniques to an advanced degree.

The first rule of negotiation is to genuinely listen to the terrorists before suggesting solutions. This is not as easy as it sounds. Many people are good at talking—usually about themselves—but not as many people are as good at listening and actually thinking about what is being said. True listening—or "staring with ears" as it has been called—will also tend to make the negotiations more peaceable.

Gestures in negotiation are important. The positioning of hands and arms shown here suggest defensiveness, and should be avoided.

Even more important, the negotiator should be careful not to start arguing with the hostage-taker. A terrorist with hostages will be in a heightened state of emotion. Anything that annoys or confuses him could lead him to hurt his hostages. Instead, what the negotiator must do is talk to the terrorist and get him to explain why he has taken this action. Once he has got the terrorist talking and relaxing, the negotiator can then act as someone whom the terrorist will trust. From this position, the negotiator can start to try to get the terrorist to surrender.

But negotiators must not be too quick to try this. If they rush the terrorist, the hostage-taker will feel that no one is really listening to his

Aircraft are a common target for terrorists. The SAS Killing House can be converted to look like the inside of an airliner for training.

Full eye contact involves focusing your eyes within this triangle.

demands, and that is when he can get dangerous. Once negotiators have heard all sides of the argument, they make up their minds whether it is within their jurisdiction to make a decision about what they are going to do. They will be faced with many questions. These will include:

- Do I feel that the terrorist will eventually surrender?
- How well-armed are the terrorists?
- Can we actually meet their demands and settle the situation peacefully?
- Is a hostage-rescue mission too risky under the circumstances?
- How tired are the terrorists? (Tiredness can make people more inclined to get aggressive.)
- Are the hostages in any immediate danger?

Once they have asked all these questions—and many more—negotiators will decide what the best course of action is. Sometimes it will involve just keeping talking to the terrorists, trying to wear them down until they are so tired and frustrated that they surrender. Other times, however, negotiators will realize that the situation is becoming too dangerous and that the hostages will need to be rescued by force.

This body language is positive. By displaying the palms of his hands, he is showing honesty and indicating that he has nothing to hide. The negotiator will often dress out of uniform.

From this moment on, the negotiator's job is to keep the terrorists talking so they are tired and confused when the hostage-rescue action begins. The negotiator will also try to find out where the terrorists are in the building. This information will be given to the hostage-rescue team. The negotiator may be the person who gives the final command that the talking is over and the hostage-rescue action should begin.

The negotiator has to be an expert in handling people. That means acquiring a number of unusual skills for telling what people are thinking. If the negotiator actually gets to see the hostage-taker, one of the best techniques is reading what is called "body language." Body language encompasses the signs that the human body gives off which tell us what is going on in a person's head. These signs are usually subconscious—this means that the person is not aware that they are doing them. Studying body language is now taught to many soldiers. A recent television recruitment advertisement for the British Army features a squad of British soldiers confronting a group of armed African civilians around a well and asking for a drink of water. For some reason, the African men become agitated and start getting to their feet and toying menacingly with their weapons. Then the officer of the British troops takes off his sunglasses, letting the leader of the other group see his eyes. The situation then calms itself, and the British soldiers are allowed to drink.

The ad was meant to show that to be a soldier requires a good understanding of negotiating skills and body language techniques—people tend not to trust someone whose eyes they cannot see. More soldiers are receiving training in aspects of reading thoughts through the way the human body behaves, and we can see how this might be valuable in negotiations.

For example, there is a sequence of body language gestures that are useful to observe in other people. Though a person's words might seem honest, their body may give away the fact that they are lying. Typical signs are:

• Rubbing the mouth or nose constantly when talking.
• Casting the eyes up when talking. People often look up when they

are using their imagination, so they could be inventing what they are saying.

• The person cannot keep eye contact. This is because the person is afraid that you will know he is lying, so he keeps his eyes away from yours.

Many of these body language signals we pick up automatically, but in hostage-taking situations, soldiers must look for them consciously to make sure they are getting the truth from the terrorist.

In addition to reading body language, negotiators can use body language to make terrorists trust them. When making a point, turning the palms of the hands up gives the impression of honesty. Eye contact should be maintained as much as possible, though staring too hard into terrorists' eyes might cause them to feel threatened. Generally the overall body language in negotiations should convey trust. If negotiators notice that the person across from them has his arms and legs crossed and that he is avoiding eye contact, this most likely means that the person is not happy with the way the

This man is leaning forward slightly, showing that he is ready to act.

conversation is going. (People tend to cross parts of their bodies in front of themselves to form protective barriers when they are feeling threatened or tense, though they also do this when they are cold!) Through recognizing body language, negotiators are able to have a better idea what the terrorist will do.

Negotiating is the first response for any hostage-rescue mission. It is far better to get everything settled without resorting to violence, because that way no one gets hurt. Unfortunately, it does not always end this way. If the hostages have to be rescued, that's when the elite hostage-rescue soldiers and police force are called into action.

RULES FOR NEGOTIATING IN A HOSTAGE-RESCUE SITUATION

- Listen carefully to the hostage-taker's demands.
- Do not threaten the hostage-taker with violence or prison, but make him aware that if he hurts anyone the consequences would be serious.
- Make surrender seem like the easy way out.
- Try to make him trust you so he feels he has someone to talk to.
- Try to find out as much as you can about the hostage-takers, including where they have come from.
- Give them rewards, such as food and drink, for releasing hostages.

GLOSSARY

Abseiling Descending a steep rock face or wall by using a double rope coiled around the body and fixed at a higher point.

CQB An abbreviation that stands for "Close Quarter Battle." This refers to warfare in confined areas like buildings, aircraft, and ships, and is taught to all elite forces.

CS gas A gas used by police and military forces to stop violent people. Though it does no permanent damage, it makes the person's eyes sting and water, and makes breathing difficult.

FBI Federal Bureau of Investigation. The FBI have their own hostage-rescue team on standby at all times.

GIGN A French counterterrorist and hostage-rescue unit. Its full name is Groupenment d'Intervention de la Gendarmerie Nationale.

GSG 9 A German police unit famed for its hostage-rescue capabilities. Its full name is Grenzchutzgruppe 9.

HRU An abbreviation for Hostage Rescue Unit.

Kevlar A very strong material used to make bulletproof vests

Olympics A worldwide sports competition held every four years, each time in a different country. The Olympics originally began in Greece in 776 B.C.

Princes Gate The name of the street in London where the SAS stormed the Iranian Embassy after it had been taken over by terrorists.

Respirator A special face mask that lets the wearer breathe normally even in places full of smoke and gas.

SAS The abbreviation for the Special Air Service, the world's most famous elite regiment.

Serrated A knife or sharp blade that is toothed or notched on the edge.

Stun grenades A special hand grenade that explodes with a very loud bang and flash, but is designed not to hurt people.

SWAT An abbreviation of Special Weapons and Tactics. SWAT teams are special American units called out to deal with hostage-rescue or other potentially violent incidents.

HOSTAGE-RESCUE UNITS OF THE WORLD

Unit: First Special Forces Battalion Counter-Terrorism Detachment
Country: Brazil
Year formed: 1983
Example of operations: Dealing with terrorist attacks and hostage-rescue operations.

Unit: M-19
Country: Colombia
Year formed: 1970
Example of operations: Helping free over 400 hostages from Bogota's Palace of Justice

Unit: FBI Hostage-Rescue Team
Country: United States
Year formed: 1984
Example of operations: Operations against a religious cult in Waco, Texas, in 1993.

Unit: Washington D.C. Emergency Response Team
Country: United States
Year formed: 1984
Example of operations: 1994. Rescuing two children from an armed man who had doused the room in gas.

Unit: Los Angeles SWAT
Country: United States

Year formed: 1965
Example of operations: A massive firefight with Middle Eastern terrorists on the streets of Los Angeles, 1977.

Unit: GSG-9
Country: Germany
Year formed: 1972
Example of operations: Rescuing 87 hostages from a hijacked airliner at Mogadishu, Somalia, 1977.

Unit: Groupe d'Intervention Gendarmerie Nationale (GIGN)
Country: France
Year formed: 1974
Example of operations: Rescuing 29 schoolchildren from a hijacked schoolbus in Somalia.

Unit: Gruppo di Intervento Speciale (GIS)
Country: Italy
Year formed: 1978
Example of operations: Fighting against the Sicilian mafia during operations in 1992.

Unit: Special Operations Militia
Country: Russia
Year formed: 1980
Example of operations: Secret

Unit: Grupo Especial de Operaciones
Country: Spain
Year formed: 1978
Example of operations: Rescuing VIPs during the 1980s.

Unit: Special Air Service
Country: United Kingdom
Year formed: 1942
Example of operations: Rescuing hostages from the Iranian embassy in London in 1980.

Unit: Israeli Special Forces
Country: Israel
Year formed: 1948
Example of operations: Assassinating Arab military leaders during the many conflicts between Israel and Arab nations.

EQUIPMENT REQUIREMENTS

SAS Hostage Rescue Outfit and Equipment—Iranian Embassy 1980

Clothing
Black assault suit
Bulletproof vest
Combat boots (black) with rubber soles

Weapons
Heckler & Koch MP5 submachine gun
Browning Hi-Power 9-mm pistol
Stun grenades
Smoke grenades
CS gas grenades

Fighting knife
Frame charges (special explosive used to blow in windows, doors, and walls)

Specialized equipment
S6 respirator
Radio set worn underneath respirator
Assault ladders
High-powered flashlight (often fitted to the submachine gun to dazzle the opponent).

RECRUITMENT INFORMATION

Federal Bureau of Investigation (FBI)
The FBI is a major organization dedicated to fighting crime and terrorism. Its activities include investigations into corruption, bribery, civil rights violations, bank robbery, extortion, kidnapping, air piracy, terrorism, and drug-trafficking matters. Working for the FBI is a demanding job, and it requires special people who are very responsible, intelligent, and self-controlled. There are many different jobs within the FBI. One of them is special agent. The entry requirements are:

- You must be a U.S. citizen, or a citizen of the Northern Mariana Islands, at least 23, and not have reached your 37th birthday on appointment.
- Candidates must be completely able to serve anywhere in the FBI's jurisdiction.
- All candidates must have good eyesight and hearing.
- Special agent applicants also must have very good hearing.
- Candidates must have a valid driver's license.
- FBI special agents must be in excellent physical condition.
- Special agents must possess a four-year degree from a college or university.

To find out more about careers in the FBI, check out the FBI website. You can find this at www.fbi.gov
The website also has some special sections for children and teachers who are interested in the FBI.

Other useful websites include:
www.fbi.gov/most-wanted.html
www.fbi.gov/publication
www.usdoj.gov/marshalls
www.safehouse.com
www.nasta1.com
www.emergency.com
www.officer.com

Special Air Service (SAS)

To enter the Special Air Service, you have to be a serving soldier in the British Army of commonwealth forces. (Sometimes other foreign nationals are considered; always check first.) You have to have a good record of soldiering and also have about three years of military service remaining.

Selection for the SAS is very tough. Courses are run twice a year, in the summer and winter. Few people make it through: of every 150 people who start the selection course, only about 15 people actually pass, sometimes fewer. For those who are considering entering the SAS, a career in the British Army is the first step. To find out about the British Army, go to any Armed Forces Recruiting Office in Britain. (They can be found in most towns and cities.) The recruiting officers tell you about the army careers on offer and help you to choose from literally hundreds of jobs and roles. For more information on the SAS, go to the following websites:

http://www.army.mod.uk

http://www.specwarnet.com/europe/sas.htm

http://www.geocities.com/alli_cool_dood/

FURTHER READING

Crawford, Steve. *The SAS Encyclopedia*. London: Chancellor, 2000.

Halberstadt, Hans. *SWAT Team: Police Special Weapons and Tactics*. Osceola, Wis.: Motorbooks International, 1994.

Katz, Samuel. *The Illustrated Guide to the World's Top Counter-Terrorist Forces*. Hong Kong: Concord, 1995.

Thompson, Leroy. *Hostage Rescue Manual*. London: Greenhill Books, 2001.

Tomajczyk, Stephen. *US Elite Counter-Terrorist Forces*. Osceola, Wis.: Motorbooks International, 1997.

Whitcomb, Christopher. *Cold Zero: Inside the FBI Hostage Rescue Team*. New York: Little, Brown & Co., 2001.

ABOUT THE AUTHOR

Dr. Chris McNab has written and edited numerous books on military history and elite forces survival. His publications to date include *German Paratroopers of World War II, The Illustrated History of the Vietnam War, First Aid Survival Manual*, and *Special Forces Endurance Techniques*, as well as many articles and features in other works. Forthcoming publications include books on the SAS, while Chris's wider research interests lie in literature and ancient history. Chris lives in South Wales, U.K.

INDEX

References in italics refer to illustrations

YUMA COUNTY LIBRARY DISTRICT